SLIME SLEEPERS

PARROTFISH

by Ellen Lawrence

Consultant:
David R. Bellwood
Distinguished Professor of Marine Biology
College of Science and Engineering
ARC Centre of Excellence for Coral Reef Studies
James Cook University
Townsville, Australia

BEARPORT
PUBLISHING

New York, New York

Credits

Cover, © Ito Fukuo/Minden Pictures; 4, © Brian Kinney/Shutterstock; 5, © Reinhard Dirscherl/FLPA; 6T, © Krysztof Odziomek/Shutterstock; 6B, © Amar and Isabelle Guillen/Alamy; 7, © Borat Furlan/Getty Images; 8T, © Subphoto/Shutterstock; 8B, © ifish/iStock Photo; 9, © Rich Carey/Shutterstock; 10, © Vanessa Devolder/Alamy; 11, © David Fleetham/Nature Picture Library; 12, © Vlad61/Shutterstock; 13, © Humberto Ramirez/Getty Images; 14, © Ito Fukuo/Minden Pictures; 15, © Rich Carey/Shutterstock; 16, © Allan Connell; 17, © atese/iStock Photo; 18, © blickwinkel/Alamy; 19, © Amar and Isabelle Guillen/Alamy; 20, © Steve Bloom Images/Alamy; 21, © Jeff Rotman/Alamy; 22L, © fullempty/Shutterstock; 22R, © Pressmaster/Shutterstock; 23TL, © paintings/Shutterstock; 23TC, © Adam Ke/Shutterstock; 23TR, © Zykov Vladimir/Shutterstock; 23BL, © Steve Bloom Images/Alamy; 23BC, © Creative Commons; 23BR, © Rich Carey/Shutterstock.

Publisher: Kenn Goin
Senior Editor: Joyce Tavolacci
Creative Director: Spencer Brinker
Photo Researcher: Ruth Owen Books

Library of Congress Cataloging-in-Publication Data

Names: Lawrence, Ellen, 1967– author.
Title: Slime sleepers : parrotfish / by Ellen Lawrence.
Description: New York, New York : Bearport Publishing, [2019] | Series:
   Slime-inators & other slippery tricksters | Includes
   bibliographical references and index.
Identifiers: LCCN 2018014422 (print) | LCCN 2018020338 (ebook) |
   ISBN 9781684027439 (ebook) | ISBN 9781684026975 (library)
Subjects: LCSH: Parrotfishes—Juvenile literature.
Classification: LCC QL638.S3 (ebook) | LCC QL638.S3 L39 2019 (print) |
   DDC 597/.7—dc23
LC record available at https://lccn.loc.gov/2018014422

For more information, write to Bearport Publishing Company, Inc., 45 West 21st Street, Suite 3B, New York, New York 10010. Printed in the United States of America.

10 9 8 7 6 5 4 3 2 1

Contents

Time for Breakfast

It's early morning on a **coral reef**.

A parrotfish is just waking up.

Its body is surrounded by a clear bubble of gooey slime.

The fish bites a hole in the slime.

Then it swims away to munch on **algae** growing on the coral.

A coral reef is made up of millions of tiny animals called coral polyps (POL-ips). When these polyps die, their skeletons are left behind, forming the rocklike reef.

a coral reef

Meet a Parrotfish

There are about 90 different kinds of parrotfish.

Some are only a few inches long.

The biggest kinds can grow to be 4 feet (1.2 m) long!

Most are brightly colored—just like a type of bird called a parrot.

Many have mouths, too, that are shaped like a parrot's beak!

bright colors

beaklike mouth

parrot's beak

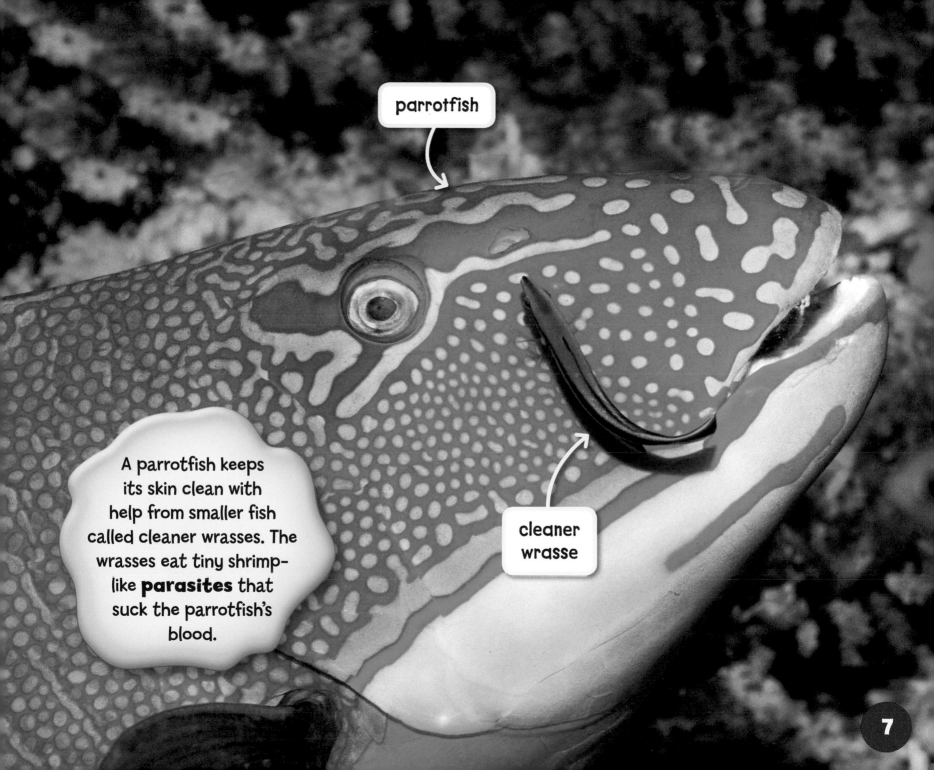

parrotfish

cleaner wrasse

A parrotfish keeps its skin clean with help from smaller fish called cleaner wrasses. The wrasses eat tiny shrimp-like **parasites** that suck the parrotfish's blood.

Feeding Time

A parrotfish has many tiny teeth that are joined together.

The teeth form a hard, beaklike mouth.

When a parrotfish is hungry, it scrapes algae from the rocky coral with its hard teeth.

As a parrotfish gobbles up algae, it also swallows lots of rocky coral.

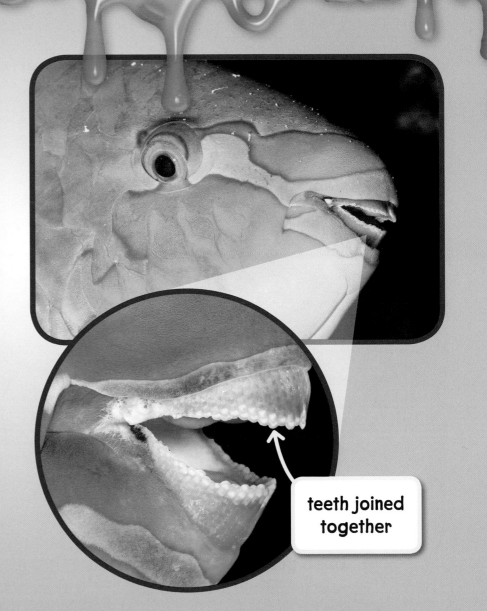

teeth joined together

Coral polyps need sunlight to live. When algae grow on coral, they block out the sun. Parrotfish eat lots of algae, which helps sunlight reach the reef!

a coral reef covered in algae

Parrotfish Poop

A parrotfish has even more teeth inside its throat!

These teeth grind up the coral into grains of sand.

Whoosh! When the fish poops, it releases a cloud of sand into the ocean.

A parrotfish can poop about 700 pounds (318 kg) of sand each year.

That's enough sand to fill a large bathtub!

a parrotfish grinding up coral

A parrotfish's sandy poop gets washed up on the shore. It forms part of a beach.

sandy poop

What do you think a parrotfish does at night?

A Slimy Coat

After feeding all day, a parrotfish finds a cozy hiding place on the coral reef.

Suddenly, soft, sticky slime oozes from the parrotfish's head.

Soon, more and more gooey slime comes out.

The slime spreads out and forms a bubble around the fish.

Then, the parrotfish goes to sleep.

A parrotfish finds a safe place to sleep.

Keep Away!

Scientists don't know why parrotfish sleep in slime, but they have some ideas.

The bubble of slime may hide a parrotfish's smell.

This might keep hungry **predators**, such as eels, from finding the fish.

Also, at night, there are no cleaner fish around to eat a parrotfish's parasites.

The slime bubble may keep the tiny bloodsuckers away from the fish.

A parrotfish's slime forms inside the fish's head in body parts called glands.

a pair of giant moray eels

Tiny Slimers

Male and female parrotfish meet up on the coral reef to **mate**.

Then, each female fish lays thousands of tiny eggs.

After a few days, baby parrotfish, called **larvae**, hatch from the eggs.

The tiny larvae swim in open water for a few weeks.

Once they are about 0.5 inches (1.3 cm) long, they make their home on the coral reef.

parrotfish eggs

A parrotfish larva eats shrimp and other tiny ocean animals. When it is about 1 inch (2.5 cm) long, it starts to feed on algae. It can also produce slime at this time.

a young bicolor, or two-color, parrotfish

Big Change!

When baby parrotfish hatch, most are females.

As they grow up, however, some of the little fish go through a big change.

These young female fish change sex.

They turn into males and live their grown-up lives as male parrotfish!

When a parrotfish changes sex, its colors change, too. A female bicolor parrotfish may be grayish blue. When she becomes a male, her scales change to a rainbow of bright colors.

a female bicolor parrotfish

Amazing Parrotfish

Some types of parrotfish live in a small group, called a harem.

All the fish in the harem are female except the male leader.

If the male fish dies, something incredible happens.

The biggest female in the group changes sex and becomes the new leader!

From making slime to changing sex, parrotfish are truly amazing.

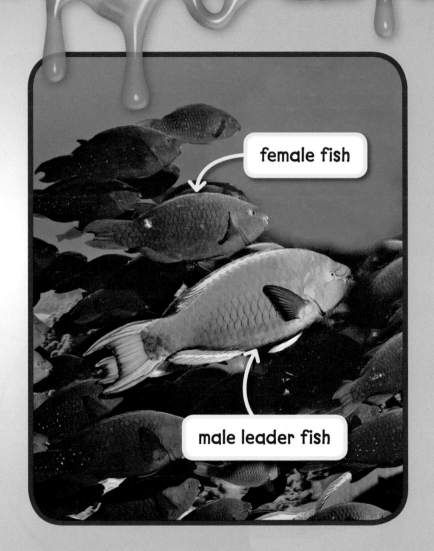

female fish

male leader fish

A parrotfish can live up to 15 years.

The name *parrotfish* describes the animal well. Can you think of another name for the fish that describes how it lives?

Science Lab

Make Slime Bubbles

Every night, a parrotfish produces a protective slime bubble. Try making a slime bubble of your very own!

1. In a bowl, mix together the white glue and baking soda. If you wish, add several drops of food coloring and stir well.

2. Add the contact lens solution to the mixture. Keep stirring until slime begins to form.

3. Take the slime out of the bowl and knead it with your hands until the slime has taken shape. Grab a straw and think about how it can be used to make bubbles in the slime.

You will need:
- A bowl
- 4 fluid ounces white glue
- ½ tablespoon baking soda
- A spoon for mixing
- Several drops of food coloring in your choice of color
- 1 tablespoon contact lens solution
- A straw

Test out your ideas. Once you've made a big bubble, answer these questions:

- **How would you describe the bubble? Is it transparent (see-through) or translucent (almost see-through)?**

- **How big is the bubble?**

- **What happens if you touch the bubble gently with your fingertips? How does the bubble feel?**

Science Words

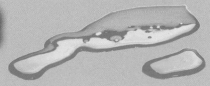

algae (AL-gee) plantlike things, such as seaweed, that mostly grow and live in water

coral reef (KOR-uhl REEF) a large mass of rock made from the skeletons of tiny animals called coral polyps

larvae (LAR-vee) the young of some animals, including fish, shellfish, and insects

mate (MAYT) to come together to produce young

parasites (PAR-uh-sites) creatures that live on or inside other living things

predators (PRED-uh-turz) animals that hunt other animals for food

Index

Read More

Borth, Teddy. *Slimy Animals (Animal Skins).* Minneapolis, MN: ABDO (2017).

Head, Honor. *Welcome to the Coral Reef (Nature's Neighborhoods: All About Ecosystems).* New York: Ruby Tuesday (2018).

Rustad, Martha E. H. *Parrotfish (Blastoff! Readers: Oceans Alive).* Minnetonka, MN: Bellwether (2008).

Learn More Online

To learn more about parrotfish, visit
www.bearportpublishing.com/Slime-inators

About the Author

Ellen Lawrence lives in the United Kingdom. Her favorite books to write are those about nature and animals. In fact, the first book Ellen bought for herself when she was six years old was the story of a gorilla named Patty Cake that was born in New York's Central Park Zoo.